The

Wild Game Birds Manual

The Wild Game Birds Manual

A Guide To Raising, Feeding, Care, Diseases And Breeding Game Birds

Alkeith O Jackson

Copyright Notice

Copyright, Legal Notice and Disclaimer

ISBN-13: 978-1502337641

Contents

Preface: Keeping and Raising Wild Game Birds as Pets

Many of the more common wild game birds, in addition to wild fowl and foreign game birds, can easily be raised in captivity. A majority of these birds, although very wild naturally, become as friendly and tame as regular barnyard fowl are. Birds are actually very intelligent, and the scratching or gallinaceous birds especially learn early on how to distinguish between those intending to persecute them and those wanting to protect them.

In many places, when they are protected from hunters, game birds will regularly feed in barnyards along with poultry, and show no fears of humans. Quail or bob-white are protected in Bermuda. They are seen quite often feeding in the roadways or in dooryards along with the chickens. When in captivity, most gallinaceous birds or wild game birds can be fed basically the same food and treated nearly the same as poultry.

For native game birds this is especially true, since many foreign species require special foods and cannot survive severe winters.

Game birds and wild fowl are not only desirable as pets and interesting to keep, but if they are raised on a large scale systematically, they can also be very profitable.

There is a growing and steady demand in many places for pheasants, quails, partridges and similar birds to stock parks and game preserves. And since most of these birds increase rapidly and lay many eggs, you can obtain a large number of them even when starting out with only a couple of birds.

The topic of breeding and raising game birds to sell is quite a broad topic and it would necessitate special work to go into all of the details.

In general, the feeding and care of game birds while raising them for profit is quite similar to what is required when raising the birds for pleasure. However, you must use larger enclosures, runs and houses. You will be wasting your time if you attempt to raise game birds for money if you don't have plenty of room for them and lots of time for devoting to your business.

It addition to their many desirable qualities for profits or as pets, many game birds also have outstanding ornamental characteristics as well. Many of them have elegant forms and are beautifully colored. Keeping a couple of the handsomer curassow, peacocks or pheasants can make a nice addition to well-maintained grounds. Visitors will always find them attractive.

Many children these days raise chickens as well as other types of fowl. However, they will get more entertainment and pleasure if they instead choose pheasants and other similar types of birds.

Any uncommon or unusual thing is always attractive, and even more so when it is very beautiful. It is hard to find any bird that is more unusual and beautiful than some pheasants and other kinds of game birds.

These birds come in so many different varieties that mentioning all of them is impossible. However, I will be describing some of the more beautiful and desirable kinds, particularly those that are easy to care for and raise and are suitable to kept by amateurs.

Introduction

Pheasants

This term is used for a number of different gallinaceous bird species. A majority of them are natives of the Orient and East Indies. In fact, the guinea-fowl, the peacock and common barnyard fowl all are pheasants. The Jungle Fowl from India is our common poultry's wild ancestors. It bears a close resemblance to some of our domestic gamecocks and bantams.

Pheasants come in many different specifies. Many have been crossed, so that there is a great amount of confusion among the most common domesticated pheasants in terms of their distinctions and names. Most so-called pheasants are quite hardy birds. The mountains and high table-lands of Asia are their natural habitats. Many of them are able to survive outdoors in the winter perfectly, even in the Northern States here.

In general there are two classes that pheasants can be grouped in: Aviary Pheasants and Game Pheasants.

Game Pheasants are suited for stocking parks and game preserves. They readily become naturalized and are able to care for themselves. Aviary pheasants are species of birds that are raised mostly for ornamental purposes. They are too tame, too tender or too valuable to be naturalized very easily or to increase and raise their young in natural conditions.

However, the two classes grade into one another. Also, although many aviary species are not well-suited for game preserves, most game pheasants do perfectly fine for pets or aviaries.

Some pheasant species make great pets. They can learn to eat from your hand, come when you call and will stay home as readily as chickens will. Other species are untamable and wild and will take to fields and woods if given the chance. Pheasants have been raised for many centuries in captivity. The early Roman and Greeks introduced them into England and Europe.

In many areas of Europe, and England in particular, pheasants are the most common game birds. Thousands of them are killed and then sold in the marketplace every year. A majority of the birds are English Ring-Necked Pheasant and English Pheasant. However, on some estates Mongolian Pheasants, Reeve's Pheasants and Golden Pheasant are well established.

Many attempts were made over the course of more than one hundred years to introduce pheasants in America. However, until 1882 they were all unsuccessful. It was then that Hon. O. N. Denny shipped around fifty Chinese Ring-Necked Pheasants from Shanghai when he was the U.S. consul-general there.

The birds were freed near Portland. Game laws strictly protected them for ten years. Then after that time, they opened a two and a half month shooting season. During that first open season, they killed more than fifty thousand pheasants. It was estimated at that time that Oregon had more pheasants than all of China.

This serves to illustrate the wonderful rapidity with which pheasants increase under favorable conditions, and their success in Oregon was so great that almost all other States have now introduced pheasants, and in many places they are very abundant.

Chapter 1

Caring For Pheasants

In breeding or rearing pheasants each person must act more or less for himself and must be governed by surroundings, locality, and other circumstances; but some general rules are suitable for all conditions. It must always be remembered that pheasants are not truly domesticated birds and that many species thrive best when their natural tendencies are catered to.

Many of the pheasants prefer to sleep in the open rather than in houses or under cover, and some species which will seek the shelter of a shed in the daytime in stormy weather will, when night comes, seek their exposed roosting place, no matter how cold or stormy it may be.

If both open and protected roosts are available, you can trust to the birds to select the place best suited to them, and you need have no fear that they will suffer from exposure, as they are perfectly well able to look out for themselves.

Chapter 2

Pens and Runs

Any sort of a place will do for the pheasant house and enclosures as long as it is well drained and somewhat hilly or sloping. A light, sandy loam soil is the best, and a clayey soil is the poorest, for it is very likely to induce disease. The pens should face the south or southwest, should have both sunshine and shade, and should extend east and west. The size of the pens will depend upon the number of birds.

For a cock and three to five hens, a good size is 6 feet high, 6 feet deep, and 8 feet wide. This will be large enough for the number of birds mentioned during the breeding months, and will accommodate twenty to thirty birds during cold weather. If your flocks increase it is better to add more pens and runs rather than to make each one larger.

The pens should be open on the southern side, with windows or doors hinged at their tops to serve as protection from cold and driving storms, and the roof should be water-tight and sloped enough to shed rain well.

Pheasants require protection from wet and dampness more than from cold weather, and a dry spot for them to run in and roost under in bad weather is the main object of the roofed shed.

The floor of the pen should be the natural earth, and it should be slightly higher than the ground around it to insure drainage. This will keep the floor dry and furnish the birds with a dust bath, which is very essential, as pheasants depend upon it to keep free from lice and to clean their plumage.

A box of old mortar, cinders, and gravel should be kept in the shed and it should be provided with good-sized perches placed well up toward the top.

Each pen should have a run or enclosure from 20 to 50 feet or more in length and the same width as the pen. This should be made of 1-inch-mesh wire netting, sunk 18 inches in the ground as a protection against rats, weasels, etc.

The top of the runs should be covered with netting, and a few inches below this top cord-netting or fish-net should be stretched to prevent the birds from injuring themselves against the wire netting if they attempt to fly out. The cover is just as necessary to keep hawks, owls, and cats out as to keep the pheasants in.

Each end of the run should have a door, and if it is possible several trees, shrubs, or bushes should be enclosed within the run, for the birds will like these much better than regular perches.

If no trees or shrubs are available, place plenty of perches in the run, and have them slightly lower than those in the shed in order to induce the birds to sleep under cover as much as possible.

In cold weather the floor of the run may be covered with dead branches, pine or fir needles, and straw, which will protect the birds' feet, while in warm weather the chips and litter will attract numerous insects, which are splendid food for the birds and will keep them busy scratching. The sides of the run may be boarded up part way if dogs or children are likely to disturb the birds, but most fanciers prefer no boarding at all.

If you keep many birds you should have enough runs so that the birds may be shut out of one and allowed in another from time to time. This will afford an opportunity to spade up the ground in the old run and to start grass, clover, or plants within it.

The change from one run to another will often add to the health of the birds, and hens that have stopped laying will often start again when placed in a new run or pen.

The runs and pens should be side by side, with communicating doors so that the birds may be transferred without handling, and all doors to the runs and pens should be arranged to close automatically with weights or springs.

All runs and pens should be kept scrupulously clean, for unclean quarters cause more diseases among pheasants than anything else. Each should be well spaded up and limed at least once a year, and at this time the runs should be planted with clover, vetch, alfalfa, timothy, or other rapid-growing, hardy vegetation to afford cover to the birds.

If the growing grass is worn or destroyed, or you cannot have it conveniently, you should place freshly cut sods or turf in the run every few days. The birds thoroughly enjoy tearing these to pieces in search of the insects they contain.

If hawks or owls are common in the neighborhood they should be destroyed, for, while these birds may eat a great many mice and other vermin and cannot reach the birds through the netting, yet they frighten them and keep them disturbed and nervous.

Rats and mice may be trapped, or a dog may be fastened to a ring which runs on a wire all along the run on the outside, and he will thus be able to guard the birds.

Minks, weasels, and other animals are at times troublesome, and to keep these out of the runs a layer of fine netting should be sunk horizontally a few inches beneath the surface of the earth outside of the run. All burrowing animals will attempt to dig close to the walls of the run, and the horizontal strip need not be over a foot wide.

Chapter 3

Tips On Handling New Birds

When your pheasants first arrive they will be timid and nervous from their trip in small crates, and every effort should be made not to frighten them. Have the crate placed in the run with a supply of water and food near at hand, and toward evening open the crate so that the birds may readily emerge. Then leave them and keep away from the run for a few days, only approaching when it is necessary to furnish food or water.

At first the birds will feel strange in their new quarters, and will try to escape at your approach, and if not treated carefully they may kill or injure themselves by dashing against the netting.

It is a good idea to place the food and water in the cage after dark for the first few days, so as not to disturb the birds, and after a short time you will find that they become accustomed to your approach.

As they gain confidence visit the run more and more often, and when you find that they are not at all nervous in your presence enter the run to place the food and water in the enclosure.

At first you should barely step inside and should increase the distance you enter very gradually until the birds will permit you to walk and work within the run without showing any nervousness or fear.

If you wish to keep the birds tame, always feed and care for them personally and try to wear the same clothes each time you enter the run. Pheasants apparently judge a person mainly by his clothing, and any great change in costume will usually startle them as much as the entrance of a complete stranger.

In the breeding-season it is particularly important not to frighten the birds, and strange people, dogs, and cats should not be permitted to approach them. You will probably find that some individuals are tamer than others, and by separating these you may be able to make them into perfect pets.

Whenever it is necessary to handle or catch a pheasant, be very careful not to grasp it by the legs, as they are very slender and easily broken. A large crotched stick with netting of string between the forks should be placed over the bird, which may be thus held down while you catch it with your hands over the wings.

Of course, this applies only to wild or nervous birds; those which are really tame and will allow you to touch them may be carefully but firmly grasped over the wings, using care not to startle or hurt them, in which case all your trouble in taming may go for naught.

Chapter 4

Breeding Pheasants

Pheasant's eggs should be hatched under common hens, and a good mother and setter of lively habits and fairly light weight should be selected for the foster parent. Cochin Bantams are the very best fowls for the purpose, and most dealers in pheasants can supply hens of this breed, especially reared for hatching pheasants' eggs.

Some fanciers prefer turkey-hens for rearing the young pheasants, but, as a rule, light-weight fowl are better. Wyandotte's,

Rhode Island Reds, and other breeds all do well. You should always make sure that the hen does not suffer from - "scaly-leg," roup," lice, or other diseases.

Dipping the hen's legs in a 5-per-cent-carbolic-acid solution before allowing her to set, repeating the treatment from time to time is a wise precaution against scaly-leg.

Lice are often fatal to young pheasants, and the hen should be well dusted with insect-powder before she is allowed to set, and once each week afterward until three or four days before the time the eggs should hatch, a good-sized dust bath should also be convenient for the hen's use.

The exact size and arrangement of the hatchery may vary a good deal, but the simpler it is the better. It may consist of several separate boxes or coops, or of a number built together in a row. The hatching coops do not require floors, but the tops should be waterproof and should slant enough to shed water readily.

Good ventilation is important, for a stuffy hatchery will become infested with lice and fleas. A 1-inch mesh wire netting or a board should extend in front of the coop for 2 or 3 feet so that the hen may eat, drink, exercise, and dust herself; and in this enclosure the chicks can run until removed to larger quarters. The run containing the hatchery should be covered and enclosed with ordinary poultry netting to keep out animals and other enemies.

A good size for the hatching-box is 14 inches square at the base, 18 inches high in front, and 14 inches high at the back.

Across the front side, at the bottom, a board 3 inches wide may be nailed with a similar strip 2 inches wide at the top. This will leave an open space about 12 inches wide, and into this space a board should be fitted and hinged to the 3-inch bottom strip, so it can open downward and outward, and a fastening should be attached to the top strip to keep the door closed when necessary.

If several boxes are used in a row, the tops, bottoms, and backs may be formed of long pieces extending the entire length of the boxes. The top of the box should project at front and back to shed rain, and if it is hinged so it can be opened it will often be found convenient.

The nest should consist of a sod, turned grass downward, with the earth side slightly hollowed out and with a little grass or short straw placed in it. If preferred, the soft earth of the box may be hollowed out and lined with soft, dry grass.

Food and water should be placed near the nest each day, and when the hen first commences to set and shape the nest, it is a good plan to use a few common hens' eggs or artificial eggs, as otherwise she may break the pheasants' eggs before she really gets comfortably settled.

Give the hen from nine to twelve eggs, according to the number she can cover, and leave her alone as much as possible. At a certain hour each day, place food and water in front of the coop and open the doors so the hen can come out.

Within twenty or twenty-five minutes she should return to her nest and may be locked up until the next day. Nests should be kept very clean; all broken eggs and other refuse should be removed, and the remaining eggs washed in tepid water if soiled.

The eggs should hatch in from twenty one to twenty-four days. If an egg has been chipped by the chick but the latter is unable to get out in eight hours it may be assisted by placing the egg in a shallow pan of warm water for a minute or two, with the chipped portion uppermost and out of water.

Never attempt to drag or pull a chick out of the shell; let it emerge slowly of its own accord. Let the young chicks remain in the nest for at least a day after the last egg has hatched and have the coops for the chicks ready for them.

These coops should be 2 feet square, 18 inches high in front, and 14 in the rear, with a runway 4 to 6 feet long, and the width of the coop with sides made of 1-inch-mesh wire netting, or of boards a foot in height.

Chapter 5

Rearing the Chicks

This is the most critical point of the young pheasants' lives, and they will require two or three weeks of unremitting care and watchfulness and attention to detail. Extreme cleanliness is necessary, and all drinking and feeding receptacles should be washed and scalded daily. Weather conditions must be noted, and precautions taken not to expose the chicks to dampness or direct and excessive sunshine, and in very dry weather the grass near the coop should be sprinkled and a leafy branch should be placed nearby to furnish shade for the chicks. Place the coop on a freshly cut grass or clover plot, and move it to a new location each day.

The tender grass shoots with the insects among the roots provide a large part of the food of the chicks. Always keep a shallow dish of water within their reach and place a few small stones in it. When they have learned the call of their foster-mother and answer it, the chicks may be allowed at large.

At first the hen may be given her freedom with the chicks, but if they show any tendency to stray away they should be confined in larger runs. Dust baths should always be furnished to the young birds, and the coops should have hinged doors like those of the hatchery boxes, so that the birds may be locked in during bad weather.

The foster-mother and the young chicks should always be given separate food. It is not necessary to feed the chicks at all until they are twenty-four hours old, but they should be given fresh, clean sand or grit to pick at during the first day.

They will develop an appetite by the second day and should be fed every two hours on this and the next two days, after which the number of feedings may be gradually reduced, until at the end of three weeks the youngsters are being fed but three times a day.

Opinions vary as regards the best pheasant food for the chicks, but many of the methods used by large breeders—such as keeping a supply of fly-blown, rotten meat on hand to produce maggots—are as disagreeable and objectionable as to be unworthy of consideration.

The best and cleanest foods for young pheasants are boiled eggs cut fine, custards, and the prepared game-bird foods. To make custard, beat ten eggs thoroughly, add a quart of milk, and bake until dry and free from whey and do not add seasoning or sugar.

Set the dish with the custard in a pan of water when baking to prevent scorching. A mixture of milk, eggs, and Indian or oat meal, just damp enough to be crumbly, is a very good food. Ants' eggs and meal-worms are excellent, and grasshoppers, small crickets, and other insects are all good.

If you rear only a few chicks you can easily raise enough meal-worms for them, and can obtain a vast number of insects by "beating" the long grass and weeds of fields and meadows. To do this, have a strong, stout net of unbleached cotton on a stout handle, and have the bag of the net at least 2 feet deep and 10 inches in diameter.

Provide several large, stout paper bags to hold the insects, and proceed to "swish" the net back and forth through the grass and weeds as you walk along.

After travelling for two or three dozen yards in this way, look into the net, and if you have found a good hunting-ground you will be surprised at the vast number and variety of insects you have caught.

Place a paper bag against the opening of the net and turn the net down into it. Grasp the neck of the paper bag over the net, and withdraw the latter slowly, gradually pressing the bag together as you withdraw the net, and thus scraping off the insects and preventing them from crawling or hopping out.

As soon as the net is fully withdrawn tie up the bag and proceed to secure more insects to fill the next bag. After all the bags are filled they may be taken home and emptied one at a time onto the ground where the young pheasants are feeding.

You will have a lot of fun watching the little fellows rushing about to capture the released insects, and the chicks will be benefited by the exercise as well. Another good idea is to hang the bags of insects in a dry place and use the dried and dead insects to mix with the eggs, custard, and mush with which you feed the chicks.

Another excellent food is made of boiled potatoes mashed and mixed with finely chopped boiled eggs, corn-meal, bran, and chopped meat scraps.

Still another desirable mixture consists of one quart corn-meal, one quart wheat middling, one pint bone-meal, one pint beef scraps, and one pint of milk thoroughly mixed.

Feed greens, such as finely cut fresh grass, clover, lettuce, chickweed, etc., in abundance. After the first few days, commence feeding whole seeds such as millet, hemp, canary seeds, etc., gradually increasing the quantity of seed and decreasing that of soft food until the diet consists entirely of seed and grain.

Be careful not to overfeed; pheasants, both young and old, are light eaters and are easily overfed. Just as soon as the birds lose interest in the food stop feeding.

Chapter 6

Feeding Pheasants

As pheasants are light feeders, a sufficient amount spent per year should be ample to pay for one pheasant's meals. Vary the food as much as possible and feed morning and evening at regular times, and do not feed any more than the birds will eat. If any feed is left over decrease the next meal by that amount.

When coming to feed the birds give a whistle or call or tap the sides or edge of the dish and the birds will soon learn to recognize the sound and run toward you. Always serve the food in clean tin, enameled, or glazed dishes, as porous earthenware is hard to keep clean.

Never scatter food on the earth or ground, as it soon spoils and is trampled into the earth. Clean up all wilted green food and scraps after each meal and keep the pens, runs, perches, and dishes as clean and neat as your own kitchen or dining-room.

Pheasants like an abundance of green food and grass, cabbage, lettuce, clover, alfalfa, apples, beets, turnips, and, in fact, any kind of fresh green growth or vegetable will be good for them.

When feeding grass dig up big pieces of coarse turf and place these in the run; these sods contain lots of insects and the birds love to tear them to pieces. Never feed long grass blades, as these catch in the birds' crops and produce a serious condition known as "crop bound," which is often fatal.

Feed plenty of grain, meat scraps, insects, cornmeal, wheat bran, and finely chopped raw or boiled beef. If you feed a mash of bran, meal, etc., never make it wet enough to be "sloppy."

Among the best grains are Kaffir-corn, paddy, oats, buckwheat, millet, and canary seed. Indian corn should be fed only in cold weather and in very small quantities, as it is very heating.

Always keep a supply of charcoal, broken oyster and clam shells, old lobster or crab shells, and gravel in the run, and invariably have a dish of clean, fresh water where the birds can drink whenever they wish.

Chapter 7

Diseases Of Pheasants

Pheasants are not subject to lots of diseases, but as they are not so long accustomed to domestication as ordinary fowl, they are more susceptible to the various ailments. Cleanliness, proper feeding, and good care do much to prevent disease; but even under the most favorable circumstances diseases will now and then trouble the birds. Disinfection is of great importance, for many of the diseases of these birds are due to minute parasites, and are easily transmitted from one bird to another.

Disinfection is of importance not only as a means of checking the spread of a disease but also as a means of preventing it; and the buildings should be occasionally disinfected as a regular matter of routine.

Buildings may be disinfected by burning sulphur, or formaldehyde fumes may be used, and the woodwork may be painted with carbolic-acid solution.

The earth in the runs and pens may be well disinfected by spading it up after top-dressing it with lime, after which cow-peas or oats or some similar quick growing plants may be sown and the run left idle for a few months. When using carbolic-acid solution add whitewash or color to it so that you may see where it has been used and will not overlook any corners or crevices.

Lice

Lice cause the most annoyance to the pheasant breeder. Great care must always be used to see that the foster-mother is not infected and, as already directed, she should be treated with insect powder to make sure. If the chicks should show signs of lice, apply Vaseline or olive-oil on the top of the heads, on the throat, around the ears, and under the wings.

Feather Pulling

This is often a serious trouble among pheasants. This affection or habit should be checked at once, and the best way to stop it is to remove the offending bird and any badly plucked birds and keep them separated from the others.

An abundance of room is a good preventive, and sometimes if plenty of cover is furnished the hens will be able to hold their own against the attacks of the cocks.

Another method is to clip the wings of the cocks and place a partition in the pen too high for them to flutter over. The hens may then escape readily to the other parts of the run or can take refuge on a high perch. If the cock's wings are clipped, low perches must be provided for their use, as they cannot fly to the high perches.

Pasting

Pasting occurs usually during the first week of life. The chick loses its vivacity, sits with eyes closed and its downy coat fluffed until it appears like a ball. Examination reveals the vent plugged or covered by a whitish, chalky, or pasty substance.

This stoppage of the vent frequently leads to death in a day or two as the result of the absorption of putrefactive poisons due to retention of the feces. Treatment consists in the immediate gentle removal of this chalky plug and the application of a few drops of sweet-oil or a bit of petrolatum.

Diarrhea

Whitish diarrhea may be caused in very young chicks by cold, by overheating, by overfeeding, or by too little or too much water. The observant fancier will come to recognize these conditions almost instinctively and will relieve them by at once altering the regime.

This should be all that is necessary. If more is required it is evident that either the case has been permitted to run so long that the chick is too weak to recuperate or infection is operating.

White diarrhea of chicks, so dreaded by the poultry man, is an affection of pheasant chicks as well. The diarrhea is merely a symptom of a severe infection of the intestines, especially of the blind pouches, or caeca, by a low form of animal life known as Coccidium tenellum, and we therefore speak of the disease as an intestinal coccidiosis.

The white coloration of the faecal discharge, as in the two previous diseases, is due to excretions from the kidneys. In certain virulent forms of the disease the minute blood-vessels on the inner portion of the intestinal wall burst, and the bleeding gives rise to a dark-brown or even blackish coloration, which obscures the white effect of the uric acid.

Treatment should begin with the administration of Epsom salts, mixing them in a mash and estimating from eight to fifteen chicks to one teaspoonful of the salts, according to age, size, and previous thriftiness.

The drinking water should contain sulphate of iron (copperas) in the proportion of ten grains of the copperas to one gallon of water, or enough permanganate of potash may be added to the drinking water to give the water a claret-red color.

The coops, feeding utensils, drinking vessels, and runs should be disinfected as previously directed. As a preventive measure, incubators and brooders should be cleansed and disinfected, and, prior to incubation, whether natural or artificial, the eggs should be dipped in 95-per-cent alcohol, or in a 4 per-cent solution of some good coal-tar disinfectant.

Gapes or Gape Disease

The disease known as gapes is particularly fatal to young pheasants. The two names given above are derived from its chief symptom.

It is caused by a worm called Syngamus trachealis, the generic name, Syngamus, recognizing the permanent sexual union that exists between the male and female. For this reason the worm is also called the branched worm, forked worm, and Y worm.

From its color it is known as the red worm. Attached to the wall of the chick's windpipe by means of the sucker on the head end of both male and female portions, it is only with great difficulty loosened by sneezing and coughed up.

Death usually results from suffocation due to obstruction of the windpipe by the large, well-fed worm distended with blood drawn from its host, or to the presence of a few worms and excessive mucus combined, or, again, to the presence of a large number of worms.

In addition to the symptom of gaping, there is a peculiar stretching out of the neck, with an actual gasping for breath. Many claim to be able to diagnose the disease by a characteristic sudden, whistling cough, somewhat like a sneeze.

However, as these symptoms might be easily counterfeited by bronchitis, pneumonia, so-called brooder pneumonia, which is really a mold infection of the lung, and roupy disease of the larynx and windpipe, the only sure means of demonstrating the disease is to find the worm.

The usual method of treatment is to take a horsehair formed into a loop, a small feather from which have been removed all barbs save those at the tip, a timothy head treated in the same manner as the feather, or even (if great care is exercised) a very thin wire twisted into a loop, pass it gently down into the windpipe, and, after making a few turns, carefully withdraw it.

Sometimes these instruments, before being used, are dipped in sweet-oil, or sweet-oil containing a few drops of turpentine. In this way the worms are either withdrawn or loosened from their attachment to the windpipe, so that the chick can cough them up. Garlic in the drinking water or mixed with the food has often proved efficacious.

Since the disease is spread by the young birds taking in with their food the worms and their eggs that have been coughed up by infected birds, one of the first steps in treatment is to remove all the birds from the infected ground and to separate the sick from the well.

The infected ground should be immediately treated so as to destroy the gape worms and their eggs.

As the earthworm has been shown to be not an intermediate host, but a carrier of the gape worm or its ova, the surest way of raising the young chicks where the ground has probably been infected is to rear them on board floors. Another method of treatment is fumigation. A smudge may be made from tobacco; tar or sulphur may be vaporized; or carbolic-acid fumes may be produced by pouring a small quantity into boiling water.

Caution must be used in the application of this method, as there is great danger of suffocating the birds or of their being overcome by the drug effect of the substances volatilized.

Cramps

Under the name of cramps, used by the keepers of pheasants, a well-known Doctor in England has described a disease which causes great mortality among birds during the second and third weeks of life.

It begins with lameness in one leg, followed the next day by lameness in the other. Death occurs, as a rule, on the third day.

Post-mortem reveals softening and fracture of the thigh-bone and of the bone of the leg, associated with the presence of considerable blood in the surrounding tissues. The only treatment is to destroy the bird, burn the carcass, and disinfect the grounds and houses.

Diseases Affecting Mainly Adult Pheasants

Roup

Certain affections known as contagious catarrh, diphtheria, and roup, if, indeed, they are distinct diseases, generally group themselves in the fancier's mind under the one name, roup.

The term diphtheria should not be used, because it belongs properly to that disease in the human family which is caused by a special bacillus which does not cause disease in birds.

The other two names may represent two different stages of the same disease, a contagious inflammation of the mucous membranes of the eyes, nose, mouth, throat, gullet, or windpipe, which may express itself by a watery, sticky, bad-smelling secretion or by the development of yellowish patches.

In the treatment of these affections the first thing is to recognize the contagiousness and to isolate the sick birds. Disinfect houses and grounds. Make a mixture of peroxide of hydrogen and boiled water, equal parts; into this plunge the head of the affected bird.

By means of a slender wire covered with a little absorbent cotton and dipped in this mixture clean out of the eye or scrape off the tongue and sides of the mouth all yellowish matter and apply a 4-percent solution of borax or boracic acid or the peroxide solution named above.

Give all birds, sick and well, a dose of Epsom salts. Keep iron sulphate or permanganate of potash in the drinking water.

Pneumonia

Pneumonia as a popular term in bird diseases probably often includes inflammation of the windpipe, inflammation of the bronchial tubes (bronchitis), and inflammation of the lungs.

Difficult breathing, wheezing, coughing, and shaking the head, associated with the usual symptoms of feverishness, weakness, and loss of appetite, call for treatment. A purgative, such as Epsom salts or a teaspoonful of castor-oil, should be given first. Keep the bird in a dry place. From time to time allow it to inhale the fumes of burning sulphur or tar, or the vapors arising from carbolic acid in boiling water. Do not allow the fumes to become too dense.

Enteritis

Enteritis, as used in bird medicine, means inflammation of the intestines. While it may originate from cold, improper feeding, and the like, it is usually an infectious disease and calls for prompt cleansing of the digestive tract, which is best accomplished by Epsom salts or a teaspoonful of castor-oil containing about fifteen drops of turpentine.

Add iron sulphate or permanganate of potash to the water; isolate the affected birds. Disinfect thoroughly the houses, utensils, and grounds, and sprinkle lime everywhere.

The causes may be coccidia, such as we find in white diarrhea of chicks; flagellates, as in the canker of pigeons; or bacteria, as in Klein's infectious enteritis.

Cholera

Cholera would really come under the third class just mentioned. The organism causing it is frequently so virulent that death comes within a few hours, even before the diarrhea symptoms have had time to manifest themselves.

The treatment would be practically that outlined under enteritis, although treatment is usually of no avail.

Kill the very sick and treat only the apparently healthy, thus anticipating and preventing the disease. Necessary in all the other diseases, it is of supreme importance in cholera to burn quickly all dead birds, after saturating them with coal oil.

Burying deep and covering with lime may have to do, but it is not so good a method. In killing the sick birds do not use the axe, and thus spatter everything with the infective blood.

Scurfy Legs

The affection known as scurfy legs, scaly-legs, scabies, or mange of the legs and feet is caused by a parasitic mite Sarcoptes mutan, which burrows under the scales and by its presence sets up an irritation which causes a rapid increase in production of cells, together with a secretion resulting in a gradual thickening and elevation of the scales.

Being a parasitic disease, scaly-legs is transmissible from one bird to another and from infested houses, perches, nests, etc.

Treatment must begin with isolation of the patient and the thorough application to the coops and fixtures of boiling soapy water, then kerosene, and finally a coat of 5-per-cent carbolic acid, to which has been added enough lime to make a whitewash.

The affected bird should have its legs soaked in warm soapsuds, this part of the treatment being completed by a good scrubbing with a small hand scrub. This alone has cured the disease. However, it is best to follow this with a good rubbing of sulphur ointment (one part flowers of sulphur to nine parts of lard, sweet-oil, or petrolatum).

Scab

Body mange or scab is caused by a sarcoptic mite, to which some authors have given the name Sarcoptes lavis. Loss of feathers at various points of the body calls for examination, which shows the skin apparently normal but the feathers broken off at the surface.

If the rest of the feather be pulled out, the roots will be seen to be covered with a dry, powdery mass made up of dead cells and parasites.

Treatment calls for isolation of diseased stock, disinfection of coop and fixtures, and application to the skin of flowers of sulphur in the form of either a dusting powder or an ointment. The application of sweet-oil containing a small quantity of kerosene or carbolic acid, carbolated petrolatum, or even lard with carbolic acid, will be found to give good results.

Air-Sac Mite

Serious disease is frequently caused in a flock by the presence of the air-sac mite. This mite, Cytodites nudus, inhabits the air-sacs of birds, chiefly those of chickens and pheasants. Often its presence in large numbers causes congestion and inflammation of the lining membrane of the air-sacs. Sometimes the bronchi become plugged with them, sometimes pneumonia is set up; sometimes the irritation opens the way for the entrance of bacteria which cause secondary disease and death.

Treatment is very difficult and unsatisfactory. Sulphur mixed in the food has been recommended. The inhalations and garlic treatment suggested under gape disease might be beneficial.

White Comb

White comb or favus is a fungus or mold disease of the comb, head, and neck. It is caused by the Achorion schonleinii. In general appearance favus resembles mange.

There is the development of white, powdery scales upon the comb, and the feathers of the head and neck become brittle and break off at the surface of the skin. The affected parts should be anointed with some oily substance like lard or petrolatum.

After a few hours, or the next morning, scrub the parts with soap and water, rinse, dry, and apply ichthyol ointment (one part ichthyol to nine parts of petrolatum). In very stubborn cases tincture of iodine may be applied.

Intestinal Worms

Pheasants frequently harbor considerable numbers of intestinal parasites. It has generally been considered that no harm results to the bird from the presence of worms in the intestinal tract.

Nevertheless, it must be recognized that the plugging of a part of the intestine by a ball of these worms or a long knotted rope composed of them must seriously derange the intestinal functions. Serious inflammation of the intestines is often caused by some of these worms.

Where it is evident that a flock is thus infested, Epsom salts should be administered at least once a month. Birds that appear markedly affected may be given one teaspoonful of castor-oil containing fifteen drops of turpentine.

Since the disease is spread by birds taking up with their food the eggs that were in* the droppings of diseased birds, the ground thus contaminated should be thoroughly disinfected.

Tuberculosis

Tuberculosis is not a subject for treatment but for eradication and prevention. It is fairly common among domesticated pheasants and is often spoken of as "going light." However, not all cases of "going light" are cases of tuberculosis.

When a bird dies of tuberculosis a post-mortem examination will reveal the liver, spleen, and intestines more or less filled with yellowish, cheesy lumps, ranging in size from that of a pin-head to that of a walnut.

Under microscopic examination these nodules or tubercles must always show the bacillus of tuberculosis, or the disease should not be called tuberculosis. There are other diseases characterized by lumps in the liver, spleen, and intestines.

For this reason the first pheasant that upon post-mortem exhibits a nodular condition of the organs should be wrapped in rags previously soaked in 5-per-cent carbolic acid, and shipped to the laboratory of the Bureau of Animal Industry, Washington, D. C, or to the State Experiment Station, for diagnosis by microscopic examination.

When the disease is discovered, isolate all "going light" birds; disinfect their droppings; if they persist in their pallor and emaciation, destroy them; disinfect all grounds and buildings; keep lime sprinkled among the droppings.

If hens are affected, but are still laying, cleanse the eggs in 95-per-cent alcohol, hatch in a previously disinfected incubator, rear in sterilized brooders, and keep the chicks absolutely apart from all other stock. In this way a new flock completely free from tuberculosis can be developed.

Chapter 8

Varieties of Pheasants

The commonest of pheasants used either as game birds or for aviaries is the Chinese or English Ring Necked Pheasant. In reality the two birds are distinct, the "Chinese" or true "Ring-Necked Pheasant" being a natural species, while the "English-Ring neck" is a cross between the Chinese Ring-neck and the old-fashioned English Pheasant, known also as the "Dark- Necked," or "Hungarian Pheasant."

When Ring-Necked Pheasants are imported from China or Oregon, they are usually fairly pure and have a distinct white ring around the neck with a purple green neck and head. The body-color is brilliant, reddish-golden brown, beautifully marked and variegated with brown, green, and buff.

The tail is long and gracefully tapered and variegated and barred with various shades of brown and copper. These colors refer to the male or cock bird, for the females or hens of all the pheasants are comparatively dull-colored with variegated brown, buff, and grayish colors.

The true English Pheasant is much like the Chinese but has no ring about the neck and is darker-colored; but every gradation and variation may be found between the two extremes.

The Mongolian Pheasant is larger than the Chinese and has a broad, white ring around the neck. The entire wing-coverts and shoulders are white, while the brown or red of the body is rich orange-red, or nearly scarlet. It is a rare bird in confinement.

The Green Pheasant or Japanese Pheasant is smaller than the Chinese and, instead of being brown or reddish, this bird is glossy, changeable blue-green below, with a green neck and breast, green and buffy back, and with wings and tail variegated with browns, buff, and green.

The Copper Pheasant is very different from any of the above and is entirely splendid copper-brown, which gleams like burnished metal, the only ornamentation being delicate lacings of white and gray.

All of these birds were introduced into Oregon and other Pacific coast states, as well as in other localities, and as they interbreed and mix freely there are a great many variations and gradations of plumage among them.

The Reeves's Pheasant is another magnificent bird, mainly golden-yellow in color, with black and white markings and an enormously long, graceful tail, which sometimes reaches a length of 7 feet.

This bird is a very hardy species and is considered a splendid game bird in Europe, where it is found wild on a good many estates. It is an excellent aviary bird, and makes a handsome and attractive pet.

The Prince of Wales Pheasant is not often seen and resembles the Chinese species in a general way but lacks the white ring on the neck and has white wing-coverts.

Elliot's Pheasant is a more beautiful species, wonderfully shaded, mottled, and variegated with white, browns, and grays. It is a desirable bird and very attractive in aviaries or with other pheasants.

Of all the pheasant family none are more brilliant or beautiful than the Golden Pheasant and the Lady Amherst Pheasant. Both of these birds are easily reared, become very tame, and make excellent pets; the golden is one of the most easily tamed of all pheasants and has a natural fondness for being petted and caressed.

Its small size, neat form, and magnificent coloring make it the most desirable of the pheasants where pet birds are desired.

The colors of the golden pheasant must be seen to be appreciated. Scarlet, blue, gold, and green are the most prominent tints, while the cape or "tippet" on the neck and the graceful, amber-colored crest add greatly to its beauty. The tail is about 2 ½ feet in length and is reticulated or mottled with red, brown, and white.

The Lady Amherst Pheasant somewhat resembles the last species and is a member of the same genus, but it differs in the arrangement of the colors and markings. The "tippet" of this beautiful bird is 3 inches deep, and composed of white and green bands, while the crest is crimson and the 3-foot tail is banded instead of being mottled as in the last species.

Another splendid species is the Silver Pheasant, a large, handsome bird mainly pure white in color, penciled with delicate lines of black, and with a graceful long tail. This species becomes so tame that it feeds and runs with the poultry; it is very hardy and is as easy to raise as an ordinary fowl.

Unfortunately, it is rather a quarrelsome and overbearing bird and should not be kept with other pheasants or small fowl.

Such are the commoner and more desirable pheasants for amateurs to keep as pets or for ornament; but the Swinhoe Pheasant with its deep-blue plumage and odd white back, the gorgeous Fiery Tragopan, the magnificent Peacock Pheasant with peacock-like eyes on tail and wings as well, are all splendid species to keep; and the big Manchurian Eared Pheasant should not be overlooked.

This peculiar bird has a queer band of white around the throat which ends in a pair of tufts or "ears," from which the bird derives its name.

The plumage is more like fur or hair than feathers, and the tail is hidden beneath great, waving, magnificent, drooping plumes. Although so handsome and unusual in appearance, the greatest value of this bird lies in the fact that it may be allowed to run at large as freely as ordinary fowls, for it is the tamest of all pheasants and never attempts or desires to return to its wild life.

Chapter 9

Other Game-Birds

The above directions as to feeding, care, and breeding apply equally well to almost any of the wild game birds or gallinaceous birds when in captivity; but in every case you must use judgment and common sense and change the details of food and care more or less in accordance with the special habits, peculiarities, or natural food of the birds you keep.

It would be a waste of time and money to build large runs and pens for one or two small game-birds, while hardy, native species, such as the quail, partridges, etc., do not require such painstaking care, when young, as do pheasants.

Always strive to learn all you can in regard to the habits, food, and peculiarities of any bird you attempt to keep, and find out as much about its natural home and food as you possibly can.

Peafowl

Peafowl are very easy to raise, for they have been long domesticated and are hardy and well able to take care of themselves. Although they are very handsome birds, yet their raucous voices and overbearing natures render them less desirable than many other ornamental birds.

Peahens will rear their own young, but as a rule they are stronger and more satisfactory when hatched and cared for by a turkey-hen or a good Brahma, Cochin, or other common fowl.

Guinea-Fowl

These are well-known birds that are natives of Africa. There are a number of species, some of them very beautifully colored. The Vulturine Guinea-Fowl, for example, is a magnificent bird and is frequently known as the Royal Guinea-Fowl.

This species has the head and upper part of throat bare of feathers, and the nape of the neck is covered with a short, velvety down. The lower parts of the neck are covered with long, slender, flowing feathers, with a broad stripe of white in the center of each feather.

This white stripe is bordered by black, dotted with white spots, and edged with blue. The breast and sides are beautiful metallic blue, the middle of abdomen black, the flanks pink, spotted with white dots encircled with black, the bill is brown, and the feet and legs brown. This is a bird that is easily reared and is a striking addition to an aviary or to a collection of ornamental wild fowl.

The ordinary Guinea-Fowl is descended from the wild bird known as the Common Guinea-Fowl, and although domesticated for many generations it has never become really tame and has altered but slightly in appearance from its wild ancestor. The commonest variety is the Pearl Guinea. It has purplish or steel-gray plumage, dotted with white, and has coral-red wattles. The ears and sides of head are white and resemble white kid.

Some varieties have a peculiar bony helmet on the top of the head, while others have a crest of feathers.

Pure white guineas are not rare and are usually merely albinos of the common variety. Other varieties are found which are white, dotted with black, and by crossing these and the white ones with ordinary birds a great number of color varieties have been produced. Guinea-fowl will cross with ordinary poultry and with turkeys, but these hybrids will not breed.

The calls of the male and female Guinea-Fowl are very distinct, that of the male being a loud shriek, while that of the female resembles the words "buckwheat!" "buck-wheat!" repeated shrilly over and over again.

Young guinea chicks are very pretty little creatures, much resembling young quail, and are quite hardy until about two months old, when the regular plumage begins to appear and the wattles on the head commence to form. At this time the birds are very delicate and difficult to raise.

Guinea-Fowl still retain many of their wild habits, and if allowed perfect freedom they will wander for long distances, will fly as well as wild birds, and will roost out-of-doors in trees.

They make their nests in secluded spots, away from houses, and desert them if any one approaches or disturbs the nests or eggs. If guineas are kept in runs or enclosures with high perches and are fed regularly at night, they will become very tame and will soon learn to come at a call.

Guinea-hens make poor setters, and the eggs should be given to a good, motherly hen or to a turkey-hen for hatching and rearing; from fifteen to eighteen eggs should be given her.

Eggs hatch in about twenty-eight to thirty days, and the young birds should be kept in covered runs until a week or two of age, after which they may be allowed to run with their foster mother in good weather.

Young guinea chicks should be fed almost as soon as hatched. They require feeding oftener than ordinary chickens, as their crops are much smaller. Indeed, a fast of several hours may often prove fatal to them. The food may be the same as that of young pheasants, and the same care should be taken to protect them from cold and dampness.

Guinea-fowl do not make very good pets, but they are useful in giving warning of strangers, enemies, hawks, etc., and are profitable when raised in large numbers for the market.

In Europe they are much used for the table, but in America they are only beginning to be appreciated. The guinea's eggs are considered better flavored and more desirable than hens' eggs, and as the birds are rather prolific layers the eggs may be used for table purposes and should prove profitable.

When allowed freedom the guinea-hens will hide their nests away, and a number of hens will lay in one nest, often filling it with thirty or more eggs.

If kept in runs or enclosures and furnished with secluded places for their nests the eggs may be gathered daily, but three to five eggs should always be left in the nest. These may be marked so as to be distinguishable.

It is a good plan to use a long-handled spoon in taking the eggs from the nest, for, if much handled, the birds may refuse to lay any more eggs there.

Quail

Many of our native quail are easily reared in captivity and become very tame. The Californian Quail, Gambel's Quail, Messina Quail, and other species are very beautiful, are easily tamed, and soon learn to eat from the hand and to come at a call. The eggs should be hatched by bantam hens, and a large amount of insect food should be fed to the chicks.

Grouse

Many species of grouse, including the European Black Grouse and the big Capercailzie may be raised in confinement, but they seldom or never become really tame or domesticated. They are mainly of interest for collections of live birds or for use in game preserves or parks.

Guans

The guans, known also as Chachalacas or Mexican Pheasants, are handsome, pheasant-like birds, found in Mexico and tropical America. They are very easily tamed and do well in captivity but seldom breed well, although they frequently lay eggs. The eggs are beautiful blue-green in color, like the eggs of a catbird or robin. They are tender birds and must be protected and kept warm in cold weather.

Tinamous

These are delicately and beautifully colored birds much like quails in habit and food. They require practically the same care as pheasants. They are quite hardy, but most varieties require protection in winter.

Sand Grouse

These are very attractive birds with pointed tails and soft, blended colors. They live naturally in barren, sandy places and are easily reared in captivity. Some varieties are quite hardy, while others must be kept m heated apartments in cold weather. Dampness and cold are fatal to these birds.

Curassows

These are large and magnificent birds about the size of a small turkey and mainly glossy, metallic black in color, often with white bellies and markings of yellow or scarlet on the rump. They have beautiful, gracefully curved crests, which are barred or mottled with white in the female birds.

In their wild state the curassows live mostly in high trees, but they will do well in runs or enclosures in captivity. They become remarkably tame and docile and make very attractive pets.

They are all natives of tropical America and must be well protected from frost and cold during our northern winters. Under favorable conditions they breed in captivity, and in the Southern States they might be bred for market or game purposes.

Chapter 10

Wild Birds

Many of our common American wild birds make excellent pets or cage-birds, and some of these are as happy and contented m captivity as when wild and are really far better off. No one should ever attempt to capture or cage any of our beautiful song-birds or insectivorous birds, for these are useful and lovely creatures that are far more ornamental and admirable in their native woods and fields than when confined in cages.

Sometimes, however, a helpless nestling will be found or an injured bird discovered, and these may be reared in cages until grown or recovered. If the young nestling is thus raised to maturity it will usually be unable to look out for itself if freed and will prefer the life in a cage to that of its wild relatives.

Many injured birds that are nursed into health by hand refuse to leave their new-found home, even when able to do so, and no one can complain if such birds prefer to remain with you of their own accord.

Our game and bird laws protect nearly all our song and insectivorous birds, and provide penalties for trapping, shooting, or confining certain species.

If you wish to keep any native birds as pets it is wise to study these laws and confine your efforts to such species as are not protected.

In this way you may be sure that you are not violating the law and may select birds to raise that are either useless, injurious, or harmful species. As most of the really interesting birds are in this class, you will find ample opportunity for securing many fine pets without decreasing the number of wild, useful, or ornamental birds.

Among the best of wild birds to rear in captivity are the crows, blue jays and other jays, nutcrackers, starlings, magpies, blackbirds, and waxwings, as well as hawks and owls.

All of these birds are easy to raise, are readily tamed, and make very interesting and attractive pets, except the hawks and owls, which seldom become very tame and are far from entertaining.

It is almost impossible to raise some species of our birds in captivity, and the flycatchers, warblers, woodpeckers, thrushes, and vireos should not be attempted. Even if they are found helpless and you wish to keep them for humanitarian reasons, you will find them very difficult subjects.

If, on the other hand, you find a deserted nestling or an injured individual of the sparrow or finch family, or a catbird, bobolink, oriole, thrasher, or any seed-eating bird, you will have little trouble in rearing the young one or in keeping the injured bird happy and healthy.

All of the finches and sparrows may be fed on seed and treated like the canary and foreign finches already described, while thrushes, blackbirds, and similar species may be treated like the soft-billed birds mentioned in a previous chapter.

Any of the young wild birds may be fed on soaked bread or cracker, hard-boiled egg, etc., just as described for the young of other cage-birds, but in each case you must use more or less judgment and have some knowledge of the natural food and habits of the bird.

Chapter 11

Care and Feeding

Wild birds in captivity require a great deal more space than those species that have been accustomed to a cage life for many generations, and even a small wild bird should have a cage as large as that required for the European Blackbird or the troupial. Many of the larger birds thrive best when given perfect freedom, and if they have a cage the door may be left wide open during the day and only closed at night to keep out cats and other enemies.

Crows, jays, magpies, etc., may be kept in this way and will come and go to their cage of their own accord. Wild birds if kept in cages should have abundant gravel, fresh water, and food daily and should be given a regular bath each day.

Most native birds are hardy and will stand a great deal of exposure and are not subject to as many diseases as domestic birds, and even when they are sick they may be doctored just as directed for regular cage-birds.

Nearly all wild birds are fond of insects, fruit, and green food, and while these are good for them, they should not be too freely given unless the bird is allowed a good deal of freedom and has abundant exercise.

Any of the standard seeds, such as canary, rape, millet, hemp, sunflower, etc., will answer for wild, seed-eating birds, and most of them will eat many common weed seeds, grains, etc.

Wild birds naturally have a far greater variety of foods than true cage-birds, and hence you should endeavor to vary their diet when in captivity as much as you possibly can.

Chapter 12

Obtaining Wild Birds

There are two ways of procuring wild birds which you wish to raise in captivity. The first is to trap them; the second, to take them from the nest when young. With few exceptions the trapped adult bird is very unsatisfactory and, moreover, in nine cases out often a bird so captured will be unhappy and unhealthy in captivity.

There is no excuse for keeping any bird or animal in a cage if the poor creature is not happy and contented, for every hour of its existence under such circumstances is torture, but many wild things seem to enjoy their new quarters from the very first, even when captured fully grown, and in such cases there is nothing cruel or inhumane about keeping them in captivity.

As a rule, it is far wiser to take young birds from the nest than to trap them, for fledglings reared by hand become very tame; they are thoroughly happy and contented in their cages, and they are far better off than when wild and exposed to the attacks of enemies of all kinds.

I have had many wild animals and birds as pets, and in every case they have been allowed perfect freedom, and I have never yet had one which did not voluntarily remain with me.

In Central America I had several tame animals which spent most of their time in the woods near my house, but they always returned at night, and the same was true of many wild birds which I have raised.

Under such circumstances no one can possibly argue that the creature is unhappy or longs for its freedom. The age at which a young bird should be taken from the nest depends a great deal upon the bird. Carnivorous birds, such as hawks, owls, etc., may be taken almost as soon as hatched, for these birds are easy to feed and are strong and hardy.

Small birds, on the other hand, should not be taken until they are well grown and nearly ready to leave the nest.

At this time they are well feathered out, can stand on a perch, and can eat and digest many kinds of food, whereas if taken too young it will be next to impossible to feed and care for them properly.

Even seed-eating birds, when very young, are fed mainly on insects, and if you once attempt to satisfy the appetite of a young bird with insects, you will have a wholesome respect for the wonderful amount of labor which the old birds perform daily in order to rear their hungry babies.

The best way to secure a young bird to rear is to find the nest and watch the young, visiting them from day to day, until you find they are able to stand upright on a perch, and can flutter their wings. In this way you can get a good idea of their habits, of the food they are accustomed to, and, moreover, both old and young birds will become familiar with your presence and when you take one of the young the parents will hardly miss it.

If on your visits you occasionally feed the young yourself, it will be far easier to rear them later on; for if the baby birds learn to associate your presence with food, they will recognize you as a friend when you carry them away with you.

Chapter 13

Rearing Young Birds

When the birds are large enough to take away, remove the one or two you have selected as being the strongest and healthiest and place the youngsters in a covered basket with a bed of soft cloth. If the bird is unable to fly you can keep it in the basket for some time, but if it can flutter and hop about, it should be placed in a cage; but a nest of soft materials should be provided, in order that the young bird may have a soft, warm spot in which to sleep until it becomes strong enough to roost overnight.

At first you will have to feed your new pet by hand. Use a medicine dropper or a spoon for giving water, and drop it into the bird's mouth.

Each time after giving the bird a drink you may hold its bill into the water cup of the cage, and very soon the little fellow will learn that he can obtain a drink in this way without waiting to have you drop it down his throat!

Feed the bird with small morsels dropped down its throat, and do not overfeed. You need have no fear that it will not notify you when hungry, and just as soon as it closes its mouth and does not open it when touched you may be sure that its appetite is satisfied for the time being.

Young birds should be fed little and often, but the amounts given and the intervals between feeding should be gradually increased.

Generally a young bird will begin to pick up food of its own accord, but it may be taught to feed earlier if you always drop a little of the food into its cup while feeding it. It requires some patience to raise a young bird by hand, but all birds grow very rapidly, and hand feeding is only required for a very short time.

As soon as your bird is able to perch, take it upon your finger and gradually accustom it to take food from your hand without your help. From this it is a very easy step to feeding from the dish, and if each time you approach the cage to feed the bird you utter a call or whistle, the bird will soon learn to respond.

If the bird is a crow, jay, magpie, or other species that is capable of learning to mimic or talk, you should commence training it just as soon as you get it from the nest.

It will not, of course, learn to talk at this tender age, but if it hears the same word or sounds every day at a certain time, they will be impressed upon its mind and it will associate them with your visits.

My own crow and jay learned to speak a few words when less than two months of age, and having once mastered the rudiments of speech these birds will learn very rapidly.

These directions and suggestions are, of course, general, and each species and individual must be fed and cared for in a slightly different manner from all others. In the following descriptions of various wild birds which are recommended for pets, more specific directions for feeding and carc are given.

Chapter 14

Hawks and Owls

These birds are very easy to rear in confinement, and from the very first they may be fed upon raw meat, liver, mice, small birds (such as English Sparrows), frogs, lizards, small fish, and insects of all kinds.

Be careful not to feed pieces that are too large, for the young hawks and owls are very greedy and will frequently choke themselves to death in their anxiety to swallow too large a piece of meat. At first, raw meat and liver are good, but these should be varied with large insects, and now and then some finely ground bone should be sprinkled on the meat.

As soon as they show any inclination to tear or peck their food, they may be given pieces of dead mice or birds, for bone is very essential to these carnivorous birds.

If fed exclusively on clear meat and insects, they will be weak and their legs will not be strong enough to support them; in other words, they will not have enough lime to form strong bones, and will suffer from the disease known as "rickets." If you cannot secure mice or other small animals, use ground bone pressed into the meat.

Most hawks and owls never become very tame, even when raised from nestlings, but certain species and some individuals show a great deal of affection and are very docile and readily tamed.

The common buzzard hawks, known as "Hen-Hawks," as well as the pretty little Sparrow-Hawks, become quite tame and will learn to come at a call or whistle, but some of the falcons are invariably wild and fierce and cannot be really tamed.

Owls are even harder to tame than hawks. The little Saw-Whet Owls, Prairie

Owls, Screech-Owls, and other small species frequently become very tame, but the larger species are usually vicious, snappy, and treacherous.

Tame hawks and owls are of little interest save as curiosities, and, as they require a great deal of space and are dirty and ill-smelling, they are not to be highly recommended as pets.

Crows, Ravens, and Similar Birds

These birds are very amusing, interesting, and entertaining pets and are exceedingly intelligent. When reared from nestlings they become as tame and docile as kittens or poultry and will voluntarily remain with their owners.

They are all capable of learning to pronounce English words and to talk or to mimic other sounds, and they may be taught many amusing tricks.

The young are easily reared by feeding hard-boiled eggs and raw egg for a few days and gradually adding insects, chopped meat, and ground bone until the birds are able to feed them-selves. The egg and meat may then be reduced and cooked meat, fruit, seeds, grain, green food, and insects given until no egg is fed.

By this time the young crows will be able to eat almost anything and will enjoy hopping about in the garden and foraging for themselves.

If you spade or dig up the ground the crows will follow you about and seize every earthworm and bug you turn up. A cage or refuge of some sort should be provided for sleeping quarters, but the birds may be given full liberty during the day if you wish.

If they are not to be allowed to roam about, you can keep them very comfortably in a large enclosure of wire netting, with a natural earth floor and growing trees, shrubs, and plants.

Crows enjoy both sand and water baths and are very clean and tidy birds. A good-sized bathtub should be furnished and a bath given daily. If kept in a netting enclosure, the birds may remain out all winter, but a shelter of some sort should be provided.

A thick mass of evergreen boughs does very well, but a water-proof box or an apartment, open at one end, fitted with perches inside is still better. In cold weather you should feed plenty of rich animal food, should give tepid water, and should be careful to see that the drinking water does not freeze so the birds cannot get at it.

Do not give baths during the cold weather but furnish a box of clean, loose, dry sand. All the crow family is born thieves and is full of mischief.

Never allow your pet crow to be alone in a room or house where there are jewels, coins, or other bright objects, for it will certainly make off with them and hide them in some out-of-the-way place where you will never find them.

Crows and their relations have powerful beaks and will kill and devour any small bird or animal they can reach, so keep kittens, rabbits, guinea-pigs, or chickens where **Jim Crow" cannot get them.

A person who has never owned a pet crow, raven, or jay does not realize how much humor a bird may possess or how entertaining a pet bird can be.

Blackbirds

Many of the American Blackbirds are very injurious to crops, and, as they are very abundant and are not good songsters, there is really no objection to keeping them in confinement.

The handsome Red-Winged or Marsh Blackbird, the Yellow-Headed Blackbird, and the Purple Crackle are all handsome, lively birds that may be easily reared and are happy in confinement.

Feed them on boiled egg and bread when young, and on a mixed diet of seeds, insects, fruit, and mockingbird food when fully grown. Some of these birds will learn to whistle or pipe a tune, like the starling, and all are very easily tamed and become very docile and affectionate. They require daily baths, great cleanliness, and large cages.

Sparrows

Many of the Native American sparrows are beautifully colored or have charming songs, and, while I do not advise keeping them in captivity as a rule, yet in many parts of the country certain kinds are kept largely as cage-birds. Among these are the Cardinal, or Virginia Redbird, the American Goldfinch, the Towhee, the Nonpareil, the Indigo-Bunting, etc.

Formerly these species were sold by all dealers in birds, but under modern laws they are mostly protected and are not offered for sale. These sparrows all require the same food and treatment as similar birds already described, and most of them thrive very well in cages.

Do not capture any of these species with the intention of keeping them in confinement, but if you find an injured or helpless bird or one that is already caged and is badly treated or improperly cared for, you are justified in caring for it properly and keeping it as a pet.

Sparrow Bird

Owl Bird

Owl Birds

Hawk Bird

Hawk Bird

Guinea Fowl

Guinea Fowl

Quail Bird

Quail Bird

Quail Bird

Peafowl Bird

Peafowl Bird

Golden Pheasant

Silver Pheasant

Diamond Pheasant

Pheasant Bird Eggs

Pheasant Bird